Auras Unraveled

Unlock Your Psychic Potential to See Auras, Detect Energy Fields, and Read Other People

Table of Contents

The information herein is offered for informational purposes solely, and is universal as so. The presentation of the information is without contract or any type of guarantee assurance.

The trademarks that are used are without any consent, and the publication of the trademark is without permission or backing by the trademark owner. All trademarks and brands within this book are for clarifying purposes only and are the owned by the owners themselves, not affiliated with this document.

Introduction

Congratulations on purchasing this book and thank you for doing so!

The following chapters will cover a brief history and understanding of auras, including common misconceptions and myths. This book will also provide techniques and exercises to see auras, how to cleanse your aura to feel renewed, the meaning associated with different aura colors and so much more. As you read on, you will discover a world that has been overlooked by many for such a long time.

There are plenty of books on this subject on the market, thanks again for choosing this one! Every effort was made to ensure it is full of as much useful information as possible, please enjoy!

Chapter 1: The Concept & History of Auras

Auras are the electromagnetic energy fields which encompass the bodies of living beings and inanimate objects. Just as how each individual is unique in their own way, so too are their auras different from one another. This ethereal radiation usually surrounds the body within the space of two or three feet.

Not everyone has the ability to see auras naturally, commonly it is psychics who claim to have that gift, and they are able to go as far as seeing the size, color, and the vibrational intensity that is generated by a person's aura. However, through practice and exercise, these energy field can be seen with the naked eye through developing your psychic abilities.

Auras are fascinating because they are able to uncover hidden information about the thoughts and feelings of a person. Auras truly allow you to read other people and give you insight into their state of being. No other element is able to do that, and that is what makes auras so unique, especially to those who possess the gift of being able to see them.

Auras are closely tied to us as individuals; they are a representation of our life force and vitality. Since we are in a constant state of flux and change, our aura will be continuously evolving and shifting. This shift depends on how the person feels, what they think and what their current state of mental/physical health may be at that time.

Since auras reflect how a person is feeling physically, mentally and emotionally, auras are often a mix of different colors depending on the frequency of these spiritual energies. Each color comes with its own definition, as this book will later explore, and the colors have their own individual definition and nature of characteristics which they represent. A person's aura is a direct reflection of them, and the healthier the person is in all aspects of health, the brighter and more vibrant their aura is going to be.

Are Auras Real?

References to auras can be traced throughout history; one of the most familiar is the idea of an aura as a glowing halo of light surrounding the head of Jesus, Mary, and the saints. This halo of light denotes the spiritual and life energy of these figures, commonly known as "Chi" and "prana" in Eastern religions.

Until recently, perception of auras was limited to clairvoyants and psychically sensitive people. However, with recent advances in technology, we are able to accurately measure these energy fields and their interactions. There is no doubt that all living beings are surrounded by electromagnetic fields, this can be easily measured by a static meter. In fact, these energy fields are used more commonly than you might imagine. For example, doctors routinely use an EKG machine to monitor the electromagnetic field of the heart.

Electromagnetic Fields can even be photographed! In 1939, Semyon Kirlian and his wife developed a method to transfer the aura of the subject to photograph by placing the subject directly on the film (such as a hand or a stone) and passing high-frequency electrical currents through it. Many years after developing this method, Kirlian was asked by a stranger to photograph two nearly identical leaves. Despite his efforts, one leaf revealed a strong energy field while the other barely registered on film. Kirlian was frustrated with his results and repeated the test several times. The next day when he shared the results with the stranger, the man told him that the leaf with the strong energy field had been plucked from a healthy plant and the barely registering leaf was picked from a diseased plant.

Do You Have a Strong Auric Field?

By now, I am sure that you are curious about what your own aura is like. That's great! It's important to understand the current state of your aura, otherwise it may be holding you back in life without your realization. Later in this book, we will discuss exactly how you can see auras and use that information. However, for now, I would like to present you with the qualities of someone who has a strong auric presence so that you can use this to gauge your own auric health. Don't worry if this doesn't sound exactly like you, auric health is a wide spectrum and the following points are presented as a rough guideline:

- You realize that it is only on very rare occasions that you find yourself feeling ill or under the weather. You don't seem to catch diseases as easily as others seem to, and you still have the energy and the drive to keep going even at the end of a long day.

- You are luckier than most other people. In fact, you could find yourself in a position where you are envied for your luck because it seems to come so easily to you in an almost inexplicable way. That is your strong aura presence drawing it towards you.

- You are a natural born leader because of your strong aura. You find that often you will be the one others turn to when it comes to taking charge of situations and being in control. At work, you are the person that your coworkers look to for leadership and guidance.

- You are a naturally positive person. No matter what obstacles may come your way, or what life throws at you, you somehow manage to pull through with your head held high, and you are still able to look at the brighter side of life. You are energetic and enthusiastic about facing challenges because you have a strong aura that surrounds you and motivates you to keep on going.

- You are able to keep an open mind, and you are not afraid of going where other people may not be ready to go. You embrace change, and you welcome it with open arms if it means the opportunity for you to become a better person.

- You are careful about the people that you let into your life. Have you ever noticed how those who have achieved success are always cautioning you to stay away from those who could inflict a negative influence into your life? There is a reason for that – being surrounded by people with a strong negative auric field will negatively affect your own.

Chapter 2: Myths & Misconceptions Unraveled

The world of auras, just like everything else, does come with its own set of myths and misconceptions which have developed over the years. To truly understand the workings of the auric world and how you can learn and benefit from it, you must be able to separate fact from fiction, and this means debunking the myths and misconceptions that surround a certain piece of information. Being able to differentiate what is real and what is not will help you better understand the world of auras and how they work, so you can use that knowledge to your benefit and improve your everyday living.

Distinguishing Fact and Fiction

There is no doubt that the subject of auras is a debatable topic because some just don't believe in its existence. Not being a believer in the subject usually stems from a lack of knowledge on the subject, which leads to not being able to fully understand it because you don't have the sufficient information needed to help you come to an informed opinion.

With that, let us take a look at some of the common myths about auras that have remained prevalent throughout the years, and we'll discover whether they are fact or fiction:

Myth #1 – A Person's Aura is Stagnant

This is a myth. Do your feelings remain stagnant throughout the day? Of course not and neither do auras. Auras reflect your state of health and mind at the present time, and if your emotions change, your aura will change along with them. If you were feeling unhappy earlier, but now you feel happy again, your aura does not remain in an unhappy color. Your aura changes with your mood and feelings.

Myth #2 – A Person's Aura Only Comes in One Color

This is a myth. People are an ever-changing race, and we come with a multitude of different personalities which change and shift as we grow from infancy to adulthood. No person remains the same throughout their entire lives, and neither do their auric colors. Because people are capable of expressing a wide range of emotions and feelings at any given time, the colors of the aura will shift and change to reflect exactly that. There is no one in the world who has one stagnant and never changing aura color about their person.

Myth #3 – Auras Are the Same Thing as Chakras

No, they are not, and that is what makes this myth number three. While auras and chakras may influence one another, make no mistake that auras and chakras are two very different things. The easiest way to differentiate between the two would be to remember that auras are a description of the energy that our bodies produce and what is emitted all around us. Auras are the energy field that surrounds our beings, and they are influenced by what happens around us. Chakras, on the other hand, are the seven gates in our bodies that control the circulation of energy. These gates, as they are known, align perfectly with how the energy flows in and through our bodies.

Myth #4 – To Cleanse Your Aura, You Would Need Special Tools and Instruments

This one is not necessarily true. Cleansing your aura does not have to be intrusive, expensive or require various tools to get the job done. In fact, all it takes are simple lifestyle changes and positive habits adapted into your life to really see and improve your aura, thereby cleansing it.

Myth #5 – Only Psychics and the Gifted Can See Auras

This is a myth. Everyone has the ability to learn how to see auras, even if they are not naturally inclined towards it. In fact, it is believed that everyone was born with the ability to see auras, only that we have become too distracted and too immersed in everything else that somewhere along the way, many of us have lost that gift.

Speculation and myth will always surround that which we do not fully understand. And with many sources of information out there, getting a clear picture and understanding of the truth can sometimes lead to misinformation. It is wise to always do extensive research on the subject you are faced with whenever you come across a point that could be myth or fact, and avoid taking anything at face value until you are absolutely sure of it.

How Chakras Are Different from Auras

Not to be confused with thinking the two are one in the same, chakras are focused on the energy that is centered inside your body, which is already one key point that makes it different from auras. Auras focus on the energies which lie outside the body, chakras focus on what lies within.

Chakras relate to different aspects of a person's life, and each chakra comes in its own different color to represent each aspect. Unlike auras which change and shift with the mood and the situation you may be going through, chakras are more rooted and stagnant. In order to see a real significant change in your chakra, you would have to undergo some massive and monumental changes in your life, changes which are strong enough to shake your chakras to the core until they reach a point where they could possibly experience transformation. Chakras cannot shift and change on a daily basis the way that auras do because chakras are more centered and focused on aspects of our life that are long term and stable.

Chakras are a reflection of the situation of your life, while auras are a reflection of your physical, mental, spiritual and emotional state of being. Chakras tell the story of your life; whereas auras tell the story of what you are feeling, thinking, going through and what your overall personality is like.

Chapter 3: Improving Your Auric Presence

Sometimes, we are so consumed by only believing and seeing what is directly in front of us that we forget there is a whole other spiritual world out there that we are completely overlooking. Whether we realize it or not, this spiritual world has not only a massive impact on our reality, but on our overall state of being.

Our spiritual and emotional states are just as important to pay attention to as our physical health; even though they may seem intangible and abstract, this doesn't make them any less important. This holds true with auras as well, they are present and having an effect on our lives whether we're aware of it or not. We've discussed how auras have different colors but it also important to keep in mind that strength and vibrational frequency are important characteristics. Dull, weak auras generally attract negativity and gloom because that's exactly what they are vibrating out into the world. If a person is constantly living in this auric state, they will not only find themselves vulnerable to depression and illness, their lives will also be filled with negative and toxic people.

Benefits of Improving Your Aura

Have you ever noticed how some people seem to have the worst luck while things always seem to work out well for others? While some of this is due to chance, a large portion of it has to do with what type of aura the person is emitting into the world. This is not to say that the difficulties of life will simply vanish, rather that where a person with a weak aura would probably be tempted to give up, a person with a strong and positive aura will keep moving forward due to their resilience and abundance of life energy. First, let's talk about why you might want to improve your aura and then we'll discuss techniques to do exactly that!

Maintaining a healthy aura will:

- Reduce stress and anxiety
- Improve your sleep
- Help guide you on your path to spiritual enlightenment
- Help you to stay happy and healthy naturally
- Cultivate more positive lifestyle habits
- Help you to gain a high and better perception of the world
- Allow you to better connect with yourself and with the universe
- Provide a basis for healing physically, spiritually and emotionally

- Provide a better quality of life overall
- Help to alleviate depression
- Help you feel grounded and stable
- Increase your feelings of vitality and joy
- Improve mental clarity

Can I Strengthen My Aura?

Yes, you can. If you can shift your state of mind from being negative to positive, you are able to strengthen, build, and improve on your aura until it is at the positive state that you want it to be, so you can reap all the benefits that it has to offer. Possessing a strong and centered aura can truly be a life-changing and magical experience. It is the reason that those who seem to radiate with energy and attract good fortune are able to do so on a daily basis; yet somehow they appear to do it almost effortlessly.

In today's world, it is very easy to feel disconnected from the universe, other people, and even yourself sometimes. This is an illusion painted by society and many have lost their connection to that raw spiritual energy inside each of us. It is through this life force and vitality that we are interconnected with all things. Even though the spiritual world isn't accessible by our physical senses, it is the tapestry of the universe and it has a massive impact on our lives. Maintaining good auric health can have a vast improvement in your life and bring with it a multitude of benefits you never would have thought possible.

Here's an expression that I'm sure you've heard at some point – that some people have a good "aura" or "presence" about them. There are just some people who can walk into a room and ooze nothing but confidence, enthusiasm, and positivity that just grabs the attention of everyone else. Have you ever found yourself thinking "there is just something about this person?", something that you can't really quite put your finger on? That's their aura at work.

These simple exercises will help you get started on improving your auric health if you want to live a more balanced life:

- **Meditate** – Yes, it is time to get back to the basics, and the best way to do that would be to meditate. I know that you've heard it a thousand times before but meditation can be life-changing. It is a great way to put things on pause, forget about your daily routine, and to take a moment to refocus and recharge yourself again. It is the first step to re-energizing a dull aura and bring it back to life again. Don't become frustrated if you difficulty with it at first, meditation needs to be practiced just like any other skill set.

- **Rest** – There is no denying that our lives are definitely more demanding today than they were before. Everything is so fast paced, fast moving that we're constantly rushing around and doing more than we can manage just to keep up. Feeling drained and tired will take a toll on your aura eventually. Our physical bodies are the expression of our life force so it is important that you make it a habit to get enough rest every day.

- **Visualize** – Find a comfortable position in your home or even out in your garden if you enjoy the sunshine, sit down, close your eyes and start to visualize. Visualize your aura, and imagine bright, happy colors are glowing and emanating around you. If it helps, think about and visualize the people and the things in your life that bring you joy until you slowly start to feel happier and happier with each thought that you think of. Filling your mind with positive emotions and thoughts will have a direct impact on the your aura.

- **Stay Away from Negativity** – The minute you feel your thoughts drifting towards the negative, immediately make a conscious effort to put a stop to it and pull them back towards more positive thoughts.

Focusing on the negative, being worried and stressed out will do nothing except dull your aura and leave you feeling miserable. The point isn't to deny your thoughts or feelings, but rather to acknowledge their presence, thank them for their input, and consciously decide that this thought or feeling doesn't serve your well being so it shouldn't be given any more attention. Watch your thought process throughout the day and make a habit of thinking about something that you're grateful for first thing in the morning before you get out of bed or do anything else.

- **Emotional First Aid** – Let's say you that have a large cut on your arm, what do you do? You should apply pressure to stop the bleeding, clean and disinfect the wound, and then you bandage it up to let it heal. We're taught these basic first aid skills to heal our physical bodies but why are we never taught similar techniques to heal emotional injuries? Do our feeling not become hurt and do they not require time to heal just as a physical wound would? To practice emotional first aid, try to remain aware of what you're feeling at any given moment (sometimes emotions change so subtly it's hard to notice) and realize that you feel the way that you do for a reason; your feelings aren't your fault. If you find yourself feeling negatively, then you owe it to yourself to take a few moments to explore that feeling. Once you can understand it then you can take the necessary steps to heal the wound. Above all, be compassionate and loving towards yourself, make sure your needs are being met, and focus on what you can be grateful for in your life.

Chapter 4: Aura Colors & What They Mean

Our auras are made up of different colors, each one symbolizing and reflecting a different meaning, part of what makes auras so unique and special in their own right. Even the intensity of the colors of your aura, especially the ones located around our head, have their own meanings and significance to them. For those with the gift and the trained ability to see a person's aura, it is a very special thing because even without the use of words, they are able to clearly see what the other person is expressing non-verbally by simply observing the colors of their aura. Your aura, in a way, is something of a natural lie detector test, because we may be able to lie with our words, but our auras will always reflect how we truly feel.

Being able to see the colors of a person's aura is indicative of what their intentions are and how they are feeling at that time. A person with a bright, clear aura full of vibrant colors, for example, is one that is filled with goodness, whereas a person with darker, more ominous colors, for example, could possibly have ill intentions. No matter how well you dress or how good you look on the outside, your aura will reveal the truth about what is really going on with you on the inside.

As mentioned earlier, a person's aura is the energy field that surrounds and emanates all around them. Everyone, whether they believe in it or not, possesses an aura that can be seen by those who have the ability and the trained eye to see them. This energy field surrounding a person is where the colors lie. Auras are made up of a combination of several characteristics, and the different spectra of colors that surround our auric state are in a constant state of flux, changing just as swiftly as our moods and emotional state do.

Auras are generally thought to have seven layers about them, and even then, each layer holds a specific meaning to it. The outer layers are thought to be more connected to a person's soul and the more spiritual side of them, whereas the inner layers of the aura are more connected to the mind, health and emotional state of being.

Can the Colors of a Person's Aura Change?

Yes, it can. In fact, you'd be surprised to know that the colors of a person's aura are capable of changing several times a day, shifting and changing just as the person is likely to do throughout the day. That change could be physical, mental, or emotional, and all of it will have an effect on the colors of the aura that surround that person at that time. The amazing thing about aura colors is that it will reflect and change with your mood because it is an extension of you. Some people even have been known to have several different colors appearing at a time because they could be feeling several different things at once.

Aura Colors and Their Meanings

Now, let's look at some of the common aura colors and what each of these colors stand for:

- **White** – Commonly represents purity, innocence, truth, and joy. White will sometimes act as undefined energy and transform into another of the other colors eventually. It can also indicate that a person is pregnant or will be soon.

- **Green** – Relates to the heart and nature. A muddy green represents an individual who is reflecting feelings of jealousy, insecurity, and sensitivity within their aura. A bright emerald green aura will appear on healers and love-centered people.

- **Yellow** – Represents life energy, inspiration, and awakening. If you notice a pale shade of yellow in the person's aura, it could mean spiritual clarity, whereas a bright shade of yellow is a representation of the person's fear of loss. A muddy yellow color, on the other hand, is a sign that the person is undergoing stress and fatigue, which means their auras are in need of some cleansing.

- **Purple** – Found in those who possess strong spiritual characteristics, including having wisdom, psychic powers, and a good intuition. An individual with violet is a visionary of the highest level; it is the most sensitive and wisest of the colors. Lighter shades of purple represent daydreaming, deep feeling, and the ethereal.

- **Red** – Courage, vitality, strength, and passion are some of the common characteristics associated with this auric color. Lighter shades of red are the ones that represent energy and sensuality, whereas a muddy red, on the other hand, means the person is having strong feelings of anger. If a person's aura has a darker shade of red about them, it is an indication that they are strong-willed and self-sufficient individuals.

- **Blue** – A reflection that the person is feeling tranquil. Individuals who are sensitive and those that are more inclined towards the creative aspects also possess some blue in their aura. Light blue reflects that the individual is feeling more at peace than anything else, while a darker or muddy shade of blue is an indication that the person is fearful of the future or of facing the truth. A deep, royal blue is found in the auras of clairvoyants and generous people.

- **Brown** – If you have this color within your aura, you are very likely a down-to-earth person with a grounded personality. Light brown auras usually indicate that the person may be feeling confused or discouraged, or perhaps even lacking confidence in themselves.

- **Orange** – A color found in those who possess the characteristics of confidence and health. Those who are sociable in nature also possess the color orange in their aura. A muddy orange color, however, is an indication that the person is lazy and lacking in ambition.

- **Pink** – A soul that is romantic and artistic, a sensual person who appreciates the finer things in life. Those who have pink auras surrounding them are people who like to love and be loved, and they like to surround themselves with family and friends who can shower them with the love that they seek. Pink auras are also a sign that the person is faithful, loyal and loving for life. However, dark pink can be an indication that a person is untrustworthy and deceitful.

- **Black** — Contrary to what you might think, black is not necessarily a reflection of evil. Those who have experienced past trauma or an illness of some sort could also hold this color within their auric spectrum. While it may not necessarily be associated with evil, black auras are still not a good thing, because it denotes that the person is full of hatred, harbors negativity or perhaps is even feeling depressed. Either way, it is never a good thing to have this color present around your auric field.

- **Silver and Gold** — Who would have thought auras would actually come in silver and gold colors too? But they do and these are very special colors! Silver symbolizes that the person has an abundance of physical and spiritual wealth about them. Gold, on the other hand, reflects that the person has divine entities who could be watching over them and keeping them safe from harm. Guardian angels ring any bells? People with some gold in their auric fields are independent individuals and are sometimes reluctant to seek help from others because they prefer to handle situations on their own.

Being able to understand what the aura colors mean is a great source of knowledge to have, especially for those who desire to have a better understanding of themselves and of other people. Aura colors are a direct glimpse into the soul of the person, reflecting all the things they are not saying aloud. All their innermost thoughts, feelings, emotions that they may have buried deep inside and tried to avoid, memories they may have forgotten about, all of it is reflected in a person's aura. It is the one place they cannot hide from. Once you are able to develop the ability to read your own aura, you'll hold the key to improving, changing and bettering your life from the inside out and drastically improve in ways you would have never even thought possible before. Once you've become skilled at reading your own aura, you will be able to apply this skill to other people and countless real life situations.

Can I Change the Colors of My Aura?
We've covered this in the previous chapter but it is so important to understand these exercises and techniques if you want to improve your aura. I can understand how difficult change is and it takes a tremendous amount of energy to get started initially. However, if you're willing to

pay the price and do the work, then you'll receive back more than you ever put in.

- Learn to let go of any stress or anxiety that is plaguing you and weighing you down. It is not always easy to let go at times, but if you are serious about changing your aura and how you feel, then you must make a conscious and consistent effort to do so. Life is too short to hold on to the things that weigh you down emotionally, so let it go and set yourself free. You will be amazed at the difference you feel when you do.

- Adopt a healthier lifestyle and incorporate some aura cleansing rituals into your routine. Exercise your mind and your body, and constantly practice empowering yourself with feelings of positivity and gratitude.

- Adopt a spiritual practice into your lifestyle routine. This one is really up to you to figure out but the main idea is to do something that connects you with yourself and your feelings. Personally, I love going for nature walks.

- Develop an understanding and awareness of the energy that surrounds you and fills you. At different intervals throughout the day, stop and take a moment to focus on how you are feeling at the time. What sort of energy resonates the strongest right then? Does the energy drain you? Or does it empower and strengthen you? Being acutely aware of how you are feeling and the energy you are emitting from yourself will help you make a conscious effort to refocus your priorities and realign yourself.

Chapter 5: How to See Auras

How would you like to be able to see the aura of another person so you can discern what their true intentions may be? Some people are gifted with being able to see auras almost immediately, while others require practice and discipline to retrain their minds on how to see what has been there all along.

We are surrounded by people, animals, and objects every day of our lives, and this means that our aura is also constantly interacting with the aura of the people and the things that we come into contact with. Not only do we expand energy through our auras, but we are also constantly absorbing the energy of what is around us, whether they be people or situations that are influencing it at that time.

Why Would I Want to Learn to Read Auras?
Because it is a talent that not many people possess. Plus, it is intriguing to find out things about the people around you that they wouldn't necessarily want to reveal on their own. Learning to read auras is like having your very own built-in lie detector test – you will always have a powerful insight into what the other person is thinking or feeling, even if they are trying to cover it up or hide it.

Being able to read people so acutely is going to be very beneficial to you because you will be able to take control of the situation at hand and guide it in the direction that you want it to go. Remember, auras reveal a person's intentions – their true intentions – for what they really are, and when you know the truth, you will be the one who is in charge and in control of the situation, not them.

Being able to read auras will also put you in better control of your own body, your health, your emotions, and everything you need to become a better version of yourself. There are some people who have even mastered the art of being able to heal themselves spiritually simply by learning how to control their auras.

And the best benefit of being able to see and read auras? To have that feeling of being more connected and in-tune with the world around you. Feel the connection not just with people, but with nature too, and everything that surrounds your everyday life.

Being able to see another's aura is a matter of reawakening that latent ability that all of us possess, and here is where we begin to explore the steps that will help you to do just that.

How to See a Person's Aura for Beginners

For beginners, developing the ability to see another person's aura could seem like an impossible feat. After all, can we really train ourselves to see something that is hidden to the naked eye because it lives on a more spiritual level? If you have never done it before, it can seem impossible. But then again, it always seems impossible until you do it, doesn't it?

People, plants, animals and even inanimate objects like rocks and buildings will have an aura that surrounds them. The true magic of auras lies in the fact that they reveal the truth more than anything else ever will, and a person's aura will tell you everything you need to know about them, even if they never verbally express or show it.

It is believed that the aura has seven layers to it, and these seven layers are known as the physical field, the etheric and mental field, the spiritual and intuitional plane, and the last two would be the celestial and the astral plane. Sounds mystical, doesn't it? Being able to read a person's aura would mean that you would also need to be able to differentiate between these seven different layers as well. When you're first starting out, the physical field is the most important because it is the easiest for a beginner to see. Focus on mastering this auric field before you worry about seeing multiple auric layers at one time.

The Physical Field — Out of all seven fields, this is the one that vibrates with the lowest aura frequency. With some practice, the physical field can become visible to the human eye even if the person has not undergone extensive training to do so. The physical field is the one which changes whenever a person's health or well-being shifts to match that state.

The Emotional Field — The emotional field, or emotional plane if you prefer to call it that, is among the most colorful and vibrant out of all the fields because — you guessed it — as the name implies, it is a reflection of our mood, emotions, and well-being. When our mood and emotions shift and change, so too do the hues of the auras that lie within this plane. The emotional field is the one that is going to be the most affected by any form of stress or tension that we may be experiencing, more so than any of the other seven.

The Mental Plane — You will find that this one tends to overlap quite a bit with the emotional plane because they are intertwined and connected with one another in some respect. Although the mental field is more spread out compared to the emotional one, in some instances it will overlap with one another. The mental field is usually a bright yellow hue, and you will have noticed they have been depicted a lot especially in historical paintings as a yellow halo appearing in the portraits of some saints. This halo is a depiction or representation of a person's aura. The aura in one's mental field can shift and change, depending on the individual's state of mind at the given time.

The Etheric Field – You know how buildings have blueprints that lay out its foundation? Well, think of the etheric plane as a blueprint for your body's physical state. The etheric plane commonly has a grey hue or appearance about it, but as a person's body starts to develop and the needs begin to change, so too does the etheric aura.

The Astral Plane – Out of the seven, this is the one that functions as a spiritual nexus between both the spiritual world and the physical world. The astral plane is the only one which exists on its own plane and is completely free from the confines and the laws which dictate time and space. The colors that are projected on the astral plane, you will find, are somewhat similar to those which are projected on the emotional plane.

The Celestial Plane – This field has the benefit of having access to all of the energies which are projected out by the universe. The celestial plane often appears to have pastel colors about it, colors which are similar in trait to the ones projected by the emotional field.

Exercises to Help You Develop Your Ability to See Auras

Here is how you can train yourself to develop the ability to see auras:

Exercise 1 – Develop an Awareness About Energy

Before you can begin to see the auras around you, you must first develop the ability to feel the energy of your life force (Chi and prana). Find somewhere comfortable and quiet where you can take a few moments to relax. Visualize a ball of white light inside of your body, just above your navel. Now, slowly, visualize the ball of light moving throughout your body and guide it to anywhere that you'd like. At first, it might feel a little silly but if you stick with it for a few minutes and keep focusing on the ball then eventually you will start to notice something happening. You should start to feel an energy or force where before was only your imagination. Soon enough, you'll be able to direct this flow of energy to anywhere in your body that you'd like, it's a very exciting feeling! You may not be able to maintain it for very long at first and that's okay. It takes a lot of energy to sustain it when you're just beginning.

Exercise 2 – Stare at A Spot

As much as we would all like to be able to see and read auras right off the bat, unfortunately, that is not the case. This is a very small and simple exercise but it will help you to become more focused and clear minded which is absolutely vital to reading auras. Begin by picking a spot and gaze at that same spot for approximately 60 seconds or so. As you are gazing at that spot, slowly allow your gaze to soften and breathe normally. Practice this soft-gaze focus and breathing several times until you have become comfortable with it and it begins to feel almost natural. The point of this exercise is to focus on the spot in an effortless matter, don't try too hard or force it. Allow it to happen gradually and fade everything else besides that spot into the background.

Exercise 3 – Taking Note of Colors
Once you have mastered energy flow and soft-gazing, it is time to move on to colors. A great method of exercising this step would be to go into a neutral colored room that has some kind of white backdrop that you can sit in front of; you can even just use computer paper as the backdrop. Find some interesting objects around your house and place them against the white backdrop one at a time. Close your eyes and focus on your breathing until you feel relaxed. Open your eyes and use the soft-gaze method on the object. Slowly, you will start to notice the field that surrounds your object and the pale colors that are emanating from it. Keep

practicing until you are gradually able to see more than one color.

Exercise 4 – Use Your Fingers

Find a room in your home that has soft lighting and make yourself comfortable in it. If there happen to be any bright lights around you in the room, ensure that they are behind you for this exercise. A white backdrop can help with this exercise as well. Once you're comfortable, join the tips of your forefingers together and start to gaze at them. Do this for about 10 seconds and then slowly move your fingers away from each other. Keep practicing this until you start to notice an invisible energy thread that has appeared between both your forefingers, an invisible link that connects them even as you draw your fingers apart slowly. Once you have perfected this on your own fingers, you may try doing this with a friend or a partner, practicing until you can see a line that connects between your fingers and theirs.

Exercise 5 – Time to Bring in A Friend

And now it is time to bring in a friend to practice with. Start in a room again with a plain colored wall and ask your friend or partner to sit about two to three feet away from the wall. Get your friend to do something that helps them relax, such as meditate or breathe deeply, because when they are more relaxed, it is easier to see their aura. Meanwhile, while your friend or partner is performing this move, you need to stand several feet away from them and start to focus on the plain colored wall behind them. With practice, you will soon start to see that there appears to be a fuzzy sort of energy field that seems to surround your friend as your slowly soften your gaze. Keep practicing, and soon you will be able to see the aura clearly.

Chapter 6: Protecting & Strengthening Your Aura

As we grow and progress throughout the different stages of our lives, our aura is affected by the changes that we undergo. Suffering a major trauma or illness of some sort, for example, can have a lasting impact on the aura which you project about you today. Spending long hours at a job you hate, or not getting enough rest or sleep will also have an effect on what happens to your aura. Negative things that happen over a period of time will eventually take a toll on your aura and drain you of the energy and vitality you once had but probably forgot about because it's been so long since you last experienced it.

How to Strengthen Your Aura Physically

Our auras are a part of us, and this means every single part of us, including the spiritual part, needs to be well cared for if you hope to strengthen your aura in the long run. Strengthening your aura physically is probably one of the easier aspects to tackle, as this can easily be done by getting enough exercise and looking after your body. Something as simple as brisk walking daily and getting in some fresh air can do wonders for your physical state of being.

When you are exercising, focus on the exercise alone and forget all the extra baggage and problems that are weighing you down. Focus all your energy on the exercises you are working on. Apart from exercising, you would also need to look after your physical state of being by getting in the right amount of nutrition, so your body is not deprived of anything.

Healthier food choices, lots of fruits and vegetables, and less sugar would be a good start. Get enough sleep and once a week, immerse yourself in an activity that induces pure relaxation, like a round of yoga or perhaps booking yourself a massage appointment. Our bodies need to recharge after a long, stressful, and busy week. They are the vessels that carry us through this world and we should respect them.

How to Strengthen Your Aura Emotionally
If there is one thing your aura is a clear reflection of more than anything else, it is your emotional state. Feelings of stress, anxiety, depression, misery or suffering from some form of emotional pain are all factors which will inevitably contribute to weakening your aura if you let them go on for a long time.

While it is true that it may be almost impossible to feel happy 100% of the time, 24-hours a day, what is possible is to train yourself to be truly happy and develop a more positive outlook no matter what life may throw your way. The first step begins by letting go of all the emotional baggage you may have been carrying around with you, and tell yourself that you are starting anew. At least emotionally, you are.

Meditation is a great tool to help you feel centered emotionally again, teaching you to practice feelings of calm and learning to let go of all the stress you may have encountered during the day. As you slowly begin to feel better about yourself emotionally, your aura will eventually follow suit and become stronger and more vibrant, which will come back around and help you feel more positive and better about yourself. Like a cycle.

Another simple thing to do to strengthen your aura emotionally is to quite simply do things that make you happy. If a walk in the park on a sunny day does the trick, go for it. If a round of shopping gives a boost to your endorphins, go on and treat yourself a little. Curling up with a good book and a delicious cup of coffee makes you feel good about yourself? Do it.

Surrounding yourself with people who radiate positivity and make you laugh is another great way to boost your emotional levels. Make it a point to immerse yourself in something that makes you feel good a couple of times a week.

We tend to get so busy and wrapped up in our daily lives that it is easy to forget we need to take some time to breathe, relax, and focus on ourselves and our spiritual state of mind too.

How to Protect Your Aura

Emotions. They can be both a blessing and curse, our strength and our weakness at the same time. The first step in protecting your aura is to do everything you can to stay away from negativity and if possible, try to avoid it completely in your life. Over time and with practice, you will soon learn how to shift your thoughts and energy towards more positive elements automatically and this, in turn, will slowly strengthen and build your aura over time until it starts to shine brighter and brighter with each positive experience you undergo that enhances your life.

Although we can't run away from negativity completely, what we can do is try our best to keep it out of our lives whenever possible. You need to be able to develop a sort of shield around yourself and your aura and use this shield to repel any negativity that you see heading in your direction.

Protecting your aura is going to involve you tapping into your visualization powers. Remember the white ball of light from exercise 1? Shielding your aura is going to require a similar process. If you haven't mastered exercise 1 already, I'd really advise you to do so. Here is the shielding technique:

First, follow the steps in exercise 1 until you can feel and direct the flow of energy within your body. Now, I want you to bring that white ball of light to the center of your body, just above your navel. Visualize the ball expanding outwards slowly, growing bigger and stronger. You want to focus in on it and pour every ounce of energy that you can muster into it. It can help to visualize something that you care deeply for or something that gives you strength, this will provide you with more energy to direct into it. Keep going until the ball is encompassing your body, protecting you completely. Once you feel like your shield is ready, then you need to visualize it becoming solid and hard. Imagine the negative thoughts and emotions from others bouncing right off it, but be sure to allow love and positivity to pass through unhindered. Spend a few minutes really picturing this. Your shield will be weak at first and disappear within a few moments but with practice you will soon be able to maintain it for as long as you wish.

Protect your aura by keeping it close to you whenever you feel that you are about to cross paths with someone or something that could potentially pollute your aura with negativity. Whenever you feel a change in your energy, it is time to change your direction and head somewhere else because the negativity has time to really make an impact on you.

Chapter 7: Seven Tips & Techniques to Cleanse Your Aura

A regular aura cleansing will help in strengthening and protecting your aura over time. Sometimes we may not even be aware that certain energies may be blocking us, and is impacting us in a way we may not even realize. Signs of this happening could include mood swings, anger, emotionally erratic behavior and even not being able to feel connected to the people around you. Whenever you feel that way, perform an aura cleansing as soon as possible to help bring some balance into your life.

Just like how we would brush our teeth or take a shower daily to keep ourselves feeling clean, auras need to be cleaned as often as possible to ensure that everything is in good working order. Think of it as a hygiene routine, but for your spiritual state instead of your physical state. You wouldn't neglect your physical state of health, so why would you do that to your aura?

Aura cleansing is more important than you realize, and because auras often go unseen, it is easy to forget that we still need to focus on doing what we need to in order to keep our auras in tip-top condition. Blockages and imbalances in our spiritual health will have adverse effects on us in the long run, and you wouldn't think about it being related to auras until you have experienced it.

How can you cleanse your aura and keep it clean? Here are a few things that you could do:

- **Smudging** – Sounds a bit weird to be smudging your aura when you should be cleansing it, doesn't it? But smudging is not exactly what it sounds like. This practice, adopted from the Native Americans, is the act of burning sage safely to cleanse the air and space around you. It is an effective way of cleansing and clearing away any negative energies that might be lingering around you, and this act of cleansing is a way of opening and welcoming more positive energy into your life. Sort of like an out with the old, in with the new concept.

- **Crystals** – Crystals are a source of positive energy and possess healing properties. You can either opt to wear the crystals as some people like to do, or you can place these crystals at certain focal points around your home as a way of surrounding your entire environment and living space with positive energy.

- **Take A Sea Salt Bath** – Do you have a bathtub? Take advantage of it and whip yourself up a nice warm bath filled with sea salt in it. Sea salt has natural cleansing properties, and you will feel so much better after a good soak. While you're soaking in the tub, rub some of that salt on your skin, and visualize yourself scrubbing away all that negativity off your body.

- **Immerse Yourself in Some Sunshine** – Remember the song that goes *"It's gonna be a bright, bright sunshiny day"*? Did you know that the sun is a natural aura booster and cleanser? Getting some sunshine into your day is a great way to leave you feeling energized, especially if you have been cooped up indoors a lot. Bright, warm rays of sunshine are a natural endorphin booster, which is why people prefer and flock to warmer weather, especially during those cold winter months.

- **Exercise Your Mind & Body** – Yoga is one of the best exercises you could integrate into your daily life because no other exercise medium combines both physical and mental training into one. Yoga has been used for years as a way to strengthen both the mind and the body, and a good aura cleanse is not just about getting rid of the energy that wears you down, but also about building and strengthening your aura so it is better able to keep those bad vibes at bay.

- **Do What Makes You Happy** – This is one of the oldest tricks in the book. There's nothing better than giving your aura the happy boost that it needs by, very simply, doing the things that make you happy. As much as negative situations around you can affect how you feel, so can doing things that lift your spirits. If you're feeling down and drained and that your aura could do with a good boost of energy and cleansing, pick an activity that you like to do and go nuts until you feel much better than when you first started.

- **See A Healer** – If all else fails, you could always opt to see a healer. Sometimes we all could use a little help feeling centered and balance again to encourage a flow of positive energy throughout our bodies. And who knows? The healers might be able to reveal something even you were not aware of perhaps. Plus, they could also give you some great tips and advice since they do this professionally.

Conclusion

Thank you for reaching the end of this book, I hope it has helped you to advance your psychic abilities and provided a solid foundation for further practice. The ability to see auras is a gift because it deepens our empathy for others and allows us to truly connect with another human without any boundaries. Our understanding of auras is rapidly expanding and I expect that we will soon see them become more established within our society. The human race is going through a period of great awakening and it is people like you who are helping to usher in a new era of peace.

Made in the USA
Middletown, DE
20 December 2018